People Skills For
New Managers

Leading By Example

I0409161

Philip Jackson

© **Copyright 2023 by PLGC Publishing - All rights reserved.**

This document is geared towards providing exact and reliable information in regards to the topic and issue covered. The publication is sold with the idea that the publisher is not required to render accounting, officially permitted, or otherwise, qualified services. If advice is necessary, legal or professional, a practiced individual in the profession should be ordered.

- From a Declaration of Principles which was accepted and approved equally by a Committee of the American Bar Association and a Committee of Publishers and Associations.

In no way is it legal to reproduce, duplicate, or transmit any part of this document in either electronic means or in printed format. Recording of this publication is strictly prohibited and any storage of this document is not allowed unless with written permission from the publisher. All rights reserved.

The information provided herein is stated to be truthful and consistent, in that any liability, in terms of inattention or otherwise, by any usage or abuse of any policies, processes, or directions contained within is the solitary and utter responsibility of the recipient reader. Under no circumstances will any legal responsibility or blame be held against the publisher for any reparation, damages, or monetary loss due to the information herein, either directly or indirectly.

Respective authors own all copyrights not held by the publisher.

The information herein is offered for informational purposes solely, and is universal as so. The presentation of the information is without contract or any type of guarantee assurance.

The trademarks that are used are without any consent, and the publication of the trademark is without permission or backing by the trademark owner. All trademarks and brands within this book are for clarifying purposes only and are the owned by the owners themselves, not affiliated with this document.

Table of Contents

Introduction

Stepping into a management role for the first time is both exciting and daunting. As you flip through the pages of this guide, you are about to embark on a journey of discovery, navigating through the world of people skills and leadership.

Nearly two decades ago, I found myself in the very shoes you might be in today. From the fast paced world of a career in hospitality to the corporate teams of a SaaS sales people, my career has taken me through a whirlwind of experiences, each shaping my understanding of what it means to be a leader. Across multiple careers spanning more than 20 years, I've felt the weight of responsibility on my shoulders, faced the ups and downs of managing people, and above all, have learned what it means to truly lead by example.

I've had the privilege (and sometimes, the misfortune) of working under a variety of managers. Some of these individuals inspired me, taught me the art of true leadership, while others... well, let's just say they showed what to avoid if I wanted to be a good leader. We often hear about the exemplary leaders, the ones who inspire and motivate. But in truth, the not-so-great ones are equally impactful. They are the contrasting shades that highlight the importance of good leadership and how not to do it.

Throughout my journey, there were countless mistakes and errors of judgement. Times when I faltered, and times when my choices paved the way for team successes that exceeded all expectations. And in these moments, both the missteps and the victories, lay the essence of growth and understanding.

I've been fortunate to cross paths with some truly visionary leaders who left a permanent mark on my leadership style. Their wisdom, guidance, and unwavering support were instrumental in shaping the manager and leader I am today. And now, with this book, I aim to be a part of your journey.

Over the next 12 chapters, we will dive into the core principles of people skills, understanding personalities, driving motivation, fostering teamwork, and so much more. This isn't just about managing; it's about leading with purpose, empathy, and resilience.

As you stand on the edge of your new role, you might be filled with a mixture of excitement and trepidation. I've been there, and I'm here to share all that I've learned, the good and the bad, to provide you with a compass as you navigate this new territory.

Let this book be your starting point, a beacon, as you embark on a journey of leadership. It is not meant to over load you with information and strategies, but rather be a jumping off point to hopefully help you avoid some of the pot holes that tripped me up along the way. The path ahead is filled with challenges and rewards, and I hope that my experiences will serve as guideposts along the way.

Welcome to the world of management. Let's lead by example.

- *Philip Jackson*

The Dual Role of Management & Leadership

If you've ever played sports, you'll recall there's always that one player everyone gravitates towards. They may not be the official captain, but their attitude, energy, and approach make them a natural leader on the field. On the flip side, there's the coach – the one strategizing, planning, and calling the shots from the sidelines. One embodies leadership; the other, management. But when you step into your first managerial role, you'll soon realize it's not an either-or situation. You'll need to be both.

Leadership and Management: Two Sides of the Same Coin

Let's start with a simple definition:

- **Leadership** is about inspiring and motivating your team to reach their full potential and achieve shared goals.

- **Management**, on the other hand, deals with the practicalities: planning, organizing, and directing resources (including people) to achieve those goals.

Consider this analogy: Leadership is like setting the destination on a GPS, while management is plotting the best route to get there.

Example: Think of a time when you were part of a group project. Remember the person who motivated everyone, ensuring everyone was excited and invested in the project's outcome? That was leadership in action. The one who made sure everyone had their parts assigned, deadlines were set, and resources were allocated? That's management.

Leading by Example: Walking the Tightrope

For first-time managers, the challenge often lies in striking the right balance. Here's how:

- **Build Emotional Connections:** Before you can lead, you need your team's trust. Be genuine. Listen actively. And, most importantly, show you care. People don't care how much you know until they know how much you care.

Example: Jenna, a first-time manager at a tech start-up, made it a point to have one-on-one coffee chats with her team members. This wasn't to discuss tasks but to genuinely get to know them, understand their aspirations, and address any concerns. It created a bond of trust and laid a strong leadership foundation.

- **Set Clear Expectations:** While motivating your team is essential, they should know what's expected of them. Clearly defined roles, responsibilities, and targets eliminate confusion and ensure everyone is on the same page.

Example: Carlos, upon taking over a design team, immediately set up a meeting to discuss the team's goals, individual roles, and how success would be measured. It ensured everyone knew their role in the larger picture.

- **Empower, Don't Micromanage:** Give your team the tools, trust, and autonomy they need to succeed. Micromanaging not only stifles creativity but can breed resentment.

Example: Instead of dictating how tasks should be done, Priya gave her marketing team the autonomy to come up with campaign strategies. They felt valued, took ownership, and the results were often beyond what Priya had envisioned.

- **Celebrate Wins, Navigate Losses:** Your team will look to you in both good times and bad. Celebrate their successes. In challenging times, don't point fingers. Instead, focus on solutions and lessons learned.

Example: After a failed product launch, instead of laying blame, Thomas called for a team brainstorming session. Together, they identified what went wrong, learned from it, and plotted a course for future successes.

- **Never Stop Learning:** To lead by example, be the example. Invest in your professional development and encourage your team to do the same.

Example: Nina, a team lead at a software company, regularly attended workshops and encouraged her team to do the same. By fostering a culture of continuous learning, her team always stayed ahead of the curve.

In Conclusion

Being a manager means you'll be juggling the roles of both leader and manager. While management deals with the 'what' and 'how', leadership is all about the 'why'. Your journey as a first-time manager will be filled with learning curves, but remember, every great leader was once a beginner. With empathy, clarity, trust, resilience, and a commitment to growth, you'll not only lead by example but inspire others to do the same.

Emotional Intelligence:

The Secret Ingredient

Emotional intelligence (often referred to as "EQ"). You've probably heard of it, right? Maybe it's that trendy buzzword you came across in a workshop or the thing your mentor raved about over coffee. Well, it's time to take a deep dive into EQ, especially as you transition into your first leadership role. Trust us, it's the difference between a good manager and a *great* one.

What is Emotional Intelligence?

Emotional Intelligence is the ability to recognize, understand, manage, and effectively use your emotions, as well as the emotions of those around you. Think of it as the 'people skills' of the managerial world. It involves:

- **Self-awareness**: Recognizing and understanding your emotions.

- **Self-regulation**: Controlling impulsive behaviours, managing your emotions in healthy ways.

- **Motivation**: Being driven to fulfil your goals.

- **Empathy**: Understanding and sharing the feelings of others.

- **Social Skills**: Building good interpersonal relationships and communicating effectively.

Real-World Applications: EQ in Action

Let's get down to the nitty-gritty with some examples:

- **Self-awareness**:
    - **Scenario**: Jenny, a young manager, finds herself getting irritated whenever her team asks too many questions during meetings.
    - **EQ Move**: Instead of lashing out or becoming passive-aggressive, Jenny takes a step back and realizes she feels this way because she thinks it reflects poorly on her preparation. By recognizing her feelings, she's better equipped to address them without causing harm.

- **Self-regulation**:
    - **Scenario**: Mike is super excited about a new project idea and wants to implement it ASAP.
    - **EQ Move**: Instead of impulsively pushing the idea, he takes a moment to weigh the pros and cons and gathers feedback from his team. This measured approach increases the project's chances of success.

- **Motivation**:
    - **Scenario**: After a string of failures, Sara's team is feeling demotivated.
    - **EQ Move**: Recognizing this, Sara reminds her team of their past successes and the bigger picture, reigniting their internal drive.

- **Empathy**:
    - **Scenario**: Tom notices that one of his team members, Alicia, who is usually bubbly, has been quiet and distant

lately.

- **EQ Move**: Instead of dismissing it, Tom reaches out privately, asking if everything is okay, showing genuine concern. This simple act builds trust.

- **Social Skills**:

  - **Scenario**: There's a dispute between two team members about the direction of a project.

  - **EQ Move**: Instead of dictating a solution, Linda arranges a meeting where both parties voice their concerns, and a collaborative solution is reached.

Why Does EQ Matter for New Managers?

As a newbie manager, you'll be dealing with people – their aspirations, their quirks, their challenges. While technical skills got you the promotion, EQ is what will make you excel in your new role. A high EQ lets you:

- Build and maintain stronger team relationships.

- Handle conflicts more effectively.

- Make informed decisions that consider the emotional climate of the team.

Boosting Your EQ

Great news! Unlike IQ, which is relatively static, EQ can be developed. Here are some tips to get you started:

- **Seek Feedback**: Regularly ask colleagues for feedback. It can provide insights into areas you may be blind to.

- **Practice Active Listening**: Really tune in when someone speaks. This means no multitasking or planning your response while they are talking.

- **Reflect Daily**: Take a few moments each day to reflect on your interactions. Were there moments you could have handled better?

Leading By Example

As a manager, you're a role model, whether you realize it or not. When you demonstrate high emotional intelligence, you set a positive example for your team. And remember, it's a journey. You will make mistakes, but with a commitment to growth and learning, you will not only become a better manager but also a more understanding and empathetic person.

So, as you embark on this new chapter of leadership, remember to pack your EQ toolkit. Your team, and future self, will thank you for it.

Effective Communication:

More Than Just Words

Welcome to the heart of people skills: communication. Managing requires more than just talk—it's about clarity, understanding team dynamics, and fostering a sense of belonging.

Why Communication Matters

Imagine this: You're managing a diverse team responsible for launching a new app. Amy from Design feels the colour scheme isn't resonating with the target audience, while Raj from Development thinks it's a minor concern. As their manager, it's your role to facilitate communication, ensuring Amy's observations are understood and Raj's technical constraints are respected.

See the challenge? In your role as a manager, you're the linchpin between different departments and perspectives. If communication breaks down, projects can fail, and team synergy can dissipate.

The Art of Listening

Before the speaking bit, let's focus on listening. Picture this: At a team meeting, Amy hesitantly voices her concerns. Instead of jumping in with solutions or brushing her off, you patiently listen, nod, and validate her perspective. This doesn't just reassure Amy; it sets an example for the entire team on how to value each member's input. Remember, a great manager listens more than they speak.

Being Clear and Concise

When conveying directives:

- **Start with the Big Picture:** Like when explaining that user experience is paramount for app success.

- **Be Specific:** If you need UI changes by Friday, state that clearly.

- **Ask for Feedback:** Perhaps Raj has a suggestion that could address Amy's concerns.

The Power of Non-verbal Communication

Say, in a team meeting, you're discussing tight deadlines. You state the importance of meeting these deadlines but lean back with a relaxed posture and an indifferent face. This conflicting message can confuse your team. Always ensure your body language aligns with your words.

Choosing the Right Medium

In our digital age, we are spoiled for choice. While an email might be suitable to send out guidelines, a face-to-face conversation (or a video call in our increasingly remote world) might be better to discuss concerns Raj and Amy have about the app.

Feedback: The Gift that Keeps on Giving

Picture receiving an update from Raj. Instead of a vague "Good work," imagine saying, "Raj, the way you implemented that feature made the app run smoother. Great job!" It's motivating and specific.

Feedback shouldn't be a one-way street. Encourage your team to share their thoughts. Maybe they'll have insights on how you can manage more effectively!

In Conclusion

Your actions set the tone for your team. By valuing open communication, actively listening, and providing precise feedback, you are not only guiding your team—you are leading by example. Just like how you'd guide Amy and Raj to collaboratively produce an app that is both visually appealing and technically sound, effective communication can lead to harmony, productivity, and empowerment.

Embark on this journey, new manager, with attentive ears and thoughtful words. Your team—and the results you achieve together—will thank you.

Building Trust & Credibility:

Your New Superpowers

Trust and credibility. Two little words, but when combined, they form the backbone of all successful relationships, especially in a professional setting. As you transition into your role as a first-time manager, building and maintaining trust with your team will be crucial. After all, trust isn't just about making sure your team believes you when you say you'll cover for them when they're running late. It's about creating an environment where they can openly communicate, feel supported, and are motivated to give their best.

Why Trust & Credibility Matter

Imagine your favourite pair of sneakers. They're reliable, comfortable, and you wear them everywhere. That is the kind of relationship you want with your team - reliable and comfortable. When trust is established, your team is more likely to:

- **Open up about challenges:** They'll come to you with problems rather than hiding them.

- **Take risks:** They'll feel safer experimenting and innovating.

- **Support decisions:** Even if they don't necessarily agree.

Building Trust: The Golden Rules

Walk the Talk: If you promise to do something, make sure you do it. Remember the time when a friend promised to help you move, but they bailed last minute? Disappointed, right? That's how your team will feel if you don't uphold your commitments.

Example: Sarah, a first-time manager at a tech startup, committed to weekly one-on-ones with her team members. She never missed a session, no matter how busy she was. This consistency built trust over time as her team saw that she prioritized their individual needs and concerns.

Listen Actively: Just because you're in charge doesn't mean you have all the answers. Listen to your team members' ideas, concerns, and feedback. When people feel heard, they feel valued.

Example: Jack, a manager at a marketing agency, started holding monthly feedback sessions where team members could share their ideas without any interruptions. Over time, the quality of project outcomes improved, and team members felt a stronger bond with Jack.

Admit When You're Wrong: Nobody's perfect. If you mess up, admit it. Apologize sincerely and make amends.

Example: Nina, a manager at a retail store, mistakenly scheduled two employees for the same shift. Instead of shifting blame, she immediately admitted the error, adjusted the schedule, and even covered a shift herself to make up for the inconvenience.

Be Transparent: Keep your team in the loop. If there's a company update or a change coming, communicate it as soon as possible. The unknown often breeds anxiety.

Example: When a software company faced potential layoffs, Ben, a team leader, kept his team informed about decisions at every stage. While the situation was tough, the transparency ensured minimal panic and misinformation.

Boosting Credibility: The Silver Lining

- **Lead with Integrity:** Your values should be clear and consistent. If you stand up for what's right and act ethically, your team will respect you for it.

- **Continue to Learn:** The best leaders are also the best learners. Join workshops, attend courses, read widely. This not only boosts your skills but also shows your team that you are committed to growth.

- **Provide Constructive Feedback:** Offering regular, constructive feedback demonstrates that you are engaged and want the best for both the individual and the team.

Example: When Mia noticed one of her designers struggling with a new software, she provided specific feedback on areas of improvement and even enrolled him in a training course. This not only improved the team's output but also solidified her credibility as a caring leader.

Remember, trust and credibility are not built overnight. It's a journey that requires patience, effort, and authenticity. By setting a strong example, you are not just managing people but leading a team that will trust and follow you through thick and thin. So, lace up those sneakers and start building those bridges. The journey is just as rewarding as the destination.

Conflict Resolution:

Leading with Understanding & Grace

Welcome to one of the most critical skills you'll ever develop as a first-time manager: conflict resolution. Let's face it—no matter how harmonious a workplace might be, conflicts are a natural part of human interaction. But fear not! Addressing conflicts with tact and confidence can not only resolve issues but can also lead to increased understanding, growth, and stronger relationships.

The Root of Conflict

Understanding the cause of a conflict is half the battle. Whether it's due to personal differences, competition for resources, miscommunication, or misunderstandings, identifying the root can aid in crafting a solution.

Example: Sarah and Mike, both team leads, are upset with each other. Sarah believes Mike is taking too many office supplies for his team, while Mike feels Sarah doesn't respect his team's needs. Here, the root conflict is resource allocation.

Active Listening

Your role is not to be the quickest problem solver but rather a mediator. Listen to each party involved, allowing them to fully express their thoughts and feelings. Resist the urge to interrupt or formulate your response while they are talking.

Example: When Jake complained about Emily always being late with her reports, instead of jumping to conclusions, their manager listened to Emily's side. It turns out her late submissions were due to outdated software slowing her down, something Jake was unaware of.

Stay Neutral

As a manager, it's crucial that you don't take sides. Being partial can lead to accusations of favouritism which further compounds the conflict.

Example: When Zoe and Liam had a disagreement about who was responsible for a project error, their manager, instead of siding with his long-time colleague Zoe, approached the situation without bias, asking both for their perspectives.

Find Common Ground

Encourage disputing parties to find commonalities. This not only reduces defensiveness but also provides a foundation for compromise.

Example: Two designers, Aria and Lucas, argued about a project's design direction. Their manager helped them realize that both wanted what was best for the client. This shared goal allowed them to collaborate on a design that incorporated both their ideas.

Propose Solutions, But Allow Them to Choose

While you can guide and suggest, it is often best for the parties involved to agree on the solution. This ensures their commitment to the resolution.

Example: After listening to both Sam and Claire's grievances about workspace noise, their manager suggested either alternating work-from-home days or investing in noise-cancelling headphones. Sam and Claire mutually decided on the headphones.

Know When to Escalate

Sometimes, despite best efforts, conflicts can't be resolved at the immediate level. Recognize when it's time to bring in HR or upper management.

Example: When a conflict between Mia and Neil began affecting team morale and neither mediation nor discussion helped, their supervisor decided it was time to involve HR.

Reflect and Learn

After resolving a conflict, take a moment to reflect. What went well? What could you have done better? Each conflict is an opportunity to refine your conflict resolution skills.

Example: After addressing a heated dispute between Alex and Casey, their manager realized he had interrupted Alex a few times. He made a note to be more mindful of this in future sessions.

In Conclusion

As a first-time manager, conflict resolution might seem daunting. But remember, every leader, no matter how experienced, started just where you are now. With time, patience, and practice, you will not only become adept at managing conflicts, but you will also create an environment where your team feels valued, understood, and empowered. So, embrace the challenge and lead by example!

Developing Your Team:

Creating a Culture of Growth

Stepping into your first management role is an exciting and often nerve-wracking experience. You've earned the title, but with that comes the weighty responsibility of leading a team. One of the most crucial aspects of this leadership journey is not just managing, but genuinely developing your team. But what does that mean, and how do you do it effectively?

Understanding The Importance of Team Development

Think of your team as a garden. Each member is a unique plant that, when nurtured correctly, will blossom. As a manager, you are the gardener, responsible for ensuring each plant gets the right amount of sunlight, water, and care.

Example: Imagine Tom, a new manager at a software company. At first, he viewed his role as strictly supervisory - ensuring tasks were completed on time. However, he soon realized that while tasks were getting done, the team's morale and overall productivity were waning. Recognizing the need for change, Tom shifted his focus from task completion to team development. The outcome? A more engaged, motivated, and high-performing team.

Getting Started with Team Development

Know Your Team Members

Start with one-on-one conversations. Understand their aspirations, strengths, areas of improvement, and what they love (or don't love) about their work.

Example: Sarah, a first-time manager at a PR firm, made it a point to have coffee with each team member during her first month. Through these chats, she discovered that Jason, who had been handling routine tasks, had a passion for graphic design. By aligning his role more with his interests, Jason became one of the firm's top contributors.

Invest in Training and Skill Development

Encourage team members to attend workshops, webinars, or courses. This not only boosts their skills but shows that you value their growth.

Example: Priya noticed that her sales team was struggling with using the new CRM software. Instead of reprimanding them, she organized a training session. This simple step improved the team's efficiency manifold.

Set Clear and Achievable Goals

Work with your team to set goals that are challenging yet achievable. Celebrate milestones and learn from setbacks.

Example: Mike set a challenging quarterly target for his marketing team. But he broke it down into monthly and weekly goals, making it easier to track and achieve. The result? The team not only met but exceeded the target.

Encourage Feedback and Open Communication

Creating a safe space where team members can voice concerns, share feedback, or pitch ideas can lead to innovation and increased trust.

Example: Jenny introduced a weekly 'Feedback Friday' where team members could share anything on their mind. This led to some game-changing ideas for the company.

Lead by Example

Your team looks up to you. Show them the importance of continuous learning, taking initiative, and being resilient through your actions.

Example: Kevin, a team lead at a finance firm, regularly shared books he was reading and courses he was taking with his team. This inspired many to take up their own learning journeys.

The Bigger Picture

Developing your team is not just about boosting productivity. It's about creating a positive work environment, ensuring job satisfaction, and fostering a culture of growth and learning. As a first-time manager, this might seem daunting, but remember, every little step counts. Your consistent efforts and genuine concern for your team's growth will not only make you a good manager but a respected leader.

Key Takeaway: Your team's growth is a testament to your leadership. Invest in them, believe in them, and watch the magic unfold!

Motivation:

The Spark That Lights Fires

As you step into your first management role, you are likely feeling a mix of excitement, anticipation, and maybe a hint of nervousness. That's all perfectly normal. Among the numerous responsibilities you'll juggle, motivating your team is a crucial one. Don't worry, though—you've got this!

The Power of Leading by Example

Imagine walking into an office where the manager is always late, disorganized, and seems disinterested. How would you feel? Probably demotivated, right? Now imagine the opposite: a manager who is punctual, organized, and genuinely cares about their work and team. The difference is stark!

Example: Sarah was the head of a startup's design team. Every day, she would be the first to arrive and the last to leave. Not because she wanted to show off, but because she was genuinely passionate. Her team noticed. When the project faced tight deadlines, instead of panicking or pushing her team harder, she rolled up her sleeves and worked alongside them. The result? Everyone felt a shared sense of purpose, and they were more than willing to go the extra mile.

Recognizing and Appreciating Efforts

This may sound simple, but a little recognition goes a long way. Let your team members know you see and value their hard work.

Example: Mike, a new manager at a tech company, initiated a 'Star Performer of the Month' recognition. But instead of just announcing the winner, he made it a point to sit down with them, discuss their accomplishments, and genuinely thank them. This not only boosted the morale of the recognized individuals but also inspired others.

Engage in Active Listening

Listening to your team's concerns and feedback can be motivating. It gives them a sense of belonging and shows you care.

Example: Tina, a store manager, noticed a decline in her team's enthusiasm. Instead of making assumptions, she organized a team lunch where everyone could openly share their feelings. By actively listening, she identified key areas of concern and worked to address them.

Be Transparent and Honest

Share company goals, updates, or any changes that might affect your team. Knowing the bigger picture can drive individuals to contribute more effectively.

Example: Jay, a project lead, always ensured that his team was in the loop about project status, client feedback, and potential changes. This transparency reduced uncertainty and built trust, encouraging his team to give their best.

Invest in Their Growth

When team members feel that their professional growth is supported, they are more motivated to contribute positively.

Example: Ria sponsored one of her most promising team members for a professional course. The team member not only upskilled but was also immensely grateful for the opportunity, which further deepened her commitment to the company.

Foster a Positive Work Environment

A pleasant, inclusive, and collaborative environment can boost morale and motivation. Celebrate small wins, promote team-building activities, and ensure everyone feels valued.

Example: Leo, a young team lead, introduced 'Fun Fridays' where the team would take a break from work for an hour, play games, or just chat. This small gesture greatly improved team cohesion and spirit.

In Conclusion

As a first-time manager, you wield the powerful ability to shape the environment and culture of your team. And there's no better way to do this than by leading by example. Remember, actions often speak louder than words. By embodying the values, work ethic, and attitude you wish to see in your team, you set a standard for excellence that inspires and motivates everyone around you.

As you continue your leadership journey, always ask yourself: "What example am I setting today?" Because every day presents a new opportunity to inspire and uplift those who look up to you.

Decision Making & Problem Solving

You're on your way to becoming a manager now. But before you get too comfy in that swivel chair, let's chat about two of the most critical skills you will need in this new role: Decision Making and Problem Solving. Think of them as the Cha-Cha of your management dance. Lead with grace, stay in tune with the music, and you'll be on your way to a standing ovation.

The Two Steps:

1. Decision Making: Think of this as choosing a direction on a roadmap. Sometimes you have a clear sign (like 'Exit here for Tacos'), other times, it's more like deciding which scenic route to take. The key is to pick a path confidently and guide your team down it.

2. Problem Solving: This is the 'Oops, roadblock ahead!' part. It's figuring out a way around that fallen tree or flooded bridge on your chosen route. Whether you reroute or build a bridge depends on your knack for finding solutions.

Step One: Decision Making Like A Pro

Listen First: Always gather input from your team. Jamie, a fresh manager at a tech startup, used to make snap decisions without consulting her team. When she decided to switch to a new project management tool, the transition was bumpy because she had not considered her team's familiarity with the old one. A simple feedback session could have prepared her better.

Consider the Big Picture: What is the long-term impact of your decision? For instance, if you're deciding whether to hire an additional team member, think about the long-term costs, benefits, and potential changes to team dynamics.

Stay Decisive: It is okay to seek advice and consider different viewpoints, but once you make a decision, stand by it. Second-guessing yourself is like trying to dance with two left feet - it's awkward and counterproductive.

Step Two: Problem Solving Like a Maestro

Encourage Open Dialogue: Let your team know they can come to you with problems AND potential solutions. Tom, a manager at a design firm, always begins problem-solving meetings with, "What can we do better?" This open-ended question encourages his team to think constructively.

Break It Down: Big problems can be daunting. But if you break them down into smaller tasks, they become manageable. Imagine trying to tackle cleaning a whole mansion; room by room feels less intimidating than the whole estate at once!

Stay Calm and Carry On: This might sound very British, but it's golden advice. If you panic, your team will panic. But if you stay calm and methodical, it will instil confidence. Remember Lucy, the manager who lost her company's big presentation file hours before the meeting? Instead of panicking, she rallied her team, and they recreated it just in time. Her calmness kept everyone focused.

Quick Tips:

- **Avoid Blame:** The blame game is a dance nobody wins. Focus on solutions, not pointing fingers.

- **Celebrate Small Wins:** Did you solve a minor problem that has been bugging the team for ages? Celebrate it! It builds morale.

- **Reflect & Learn:** After a major decision or problem-solving exercise, reflect on what went well and what you would change for next time.

Remember, every manager, from the CEO of a Fortune 500 to the supervisor at the local coffee shop, has faced decisions and problems that tested their mettle. What sets a great leader apart is the grace with which they handle these challenges and the examples they set while doing so.

Time Management & Prioritization:

Leading An Efficient Team

Stepping into a managerial role for the first time can feel a lot like juggling. Suddenly, there are more balls in the air than you're used to. The secret to keeping them all up? Mastering time management and prioritization. And as a leader, how you manage your time doesn't just impact you—it sets the pace and tone for your entire team.

The Power of Prioritization

Imagine this: Jack, a new manager at a trendy shoe company, starts his day without a clear plan. He reacts to emails as they come, takes impromptu meetings, and hops between tasks. By the end of the day, he feels swamped and yet, very little has been accomplished.

Conversely, Maya, another first-time manager at a competitor shoe brand, starts her day listing her top 3 priorities. She sets specific blocks of time for meetings, focused work, and even short breaks. At day's end, not only has she ticked off her priority list, but she also feels energized rather than drained.

Lesson: It's not about how busy you are, but how productive you are.

Tackling the Time Management Beast

The Eisenhower Box: This simple matrix can help you decide on and prioritize tasks by urgency and importance. Things that are both urgent and important take top priority, while neither urgent nor important tasks might be delegated or scheduled for a later time.

Example: Sarah, a manager at a digital agency, uses the Eisenhower Box every morning. It helps her decide which client projects need immediate attention, which tasks she can delegate to her team, and which meetings she can reschedule.

Time-blocking: Instead of working in a reactive mode, divide your day into blocks of time. Dedicate each block to a specific task or activity and stick to it.

Example: Tom, a newly minted manager at a café, allots specific times for inventory checks, team feedback sessions, and administrative work. This ensures he doesn't neglect any aspect of his role.

Learn to say 'No': Not every task or meeting requires your attention. Being discerning about where you spend your time is crucial.

Example: When Ria, a manager at a publishing house, was invited to every book launch, she initially tried to attend them all. She quickly realized that her presence was more essential at internal strategy meetings than at every external event. She became selective, freeing up time for crucial responsibilities.

Setting the Right Example

Time management isn't just a personal productivity tool. When your team sees you prioritizing tasks efficiently, it encourages them to do the same.

Example: Leo, a first-time manager at a tech firm, was transparent about his work methods. He often shared his strategies for time management with his team. Over time, not only did Leo's productivity soar, but his entire team became more efficient, emulating his methods.

In Conclusion

Remember, time is a finite resource. You cannot make more of it, but with the right strategies, you can make the most of it. As you transition into your managerial role, remember that mastering time management and prioritization is not just for your benefit. It's about setting the right tone, pace, and example for your team. Embrace these tools, and watch as efficiency becomes a defining trait of your leadership style.

Diversity & Inclusion:

Leading with Empathy

"It is time for parents to teach young people early on that in diversity there is beauty and there is strength." – Maya Angelou

By making it to chapter 10, you are well on your way to becoming an exceptional first-time manager. We have discussed various aspects of people skills, and today, we tackle one of the most crucial elements of contemporary leadership: Diversity and Inclusion (D&I).

Understanding Diversity & Inclusion

Let's start with the basics. *Diversity* refers to the variety of differences among people, including gender, race, age, sexual orientation, cultural background, and more. *Inclusion*, on the other hand, is about creating an environment where diverse individuals feel valued, respected, and have equal access to opportunities.

Why Does D&I Matter?

Embracing D&I not only reflects the right values, but it is also beneficial for organizations:

- **Diverse Teams Innovate Better:** A team with different backgrounds brings unique ideas, leading to better problem-solving.

- **Improved Employee Satisfaction:** Employees feel more engaged when they believe their unique voices are heard and respected.

- **Attracting Top Talent:** Companies recognized for their D&I efforts are more appealing to potential hires.

Example: *Imagine your team is developing a product for a global audience. With a diverse team, you can gain insights from various cultural perspectives, ensuring the product resonates with people worldwide.*

Leading by Example in D&I

As a manager, how you approach D&I sets the tone for your team.

- **Educate Yourself:** It is okay not to know everything. Attend workshops, read, or even take online courses about D&I. The key is to remain open-minded and willing to learn.

- **Promote Open Dialogue:** Create safe spaces where team members can share experiences or concerns related to diversity. Be an active listener and encourage others to do the same.

- **Challenge Biases:** Everyone has biases. Recognizing and confronting them is crucial. When making decisions, especially about promotions or hiring, always question if bias plays a part.

- **Hire Diversely:** Don't just speak about diversity; implement it. Ensure your hiring practices give everyone a fair chance.

Example: Sarah, a young manager, noticed that all her recent hires were very similar in background and thought. She then decided to collaborate with HR, implementing blind recruitment practices where names and universities were hidden during initial CV screenings. This led to a more varied pool of candidates.

- **Celebrate Differences:** Recognize cultural holidays, host international potlucks, or even run sessions where team members can share about their backgrounds.

- **Mentor and Advocate:** It's not enough to bring diverse talent into your team; you also need to support their growth and ensure they have equal opportunities.

Example: Raj, a new team member from India, had brilliant ideas but hesitated to voice them during meetings. Recognizing this, his manager, Jane, regularly asked for Raj's input and even set up a mentorship program to boost his confidence.

Potential Pitfalls & How to Avoid Them

- **Tokenism:** This means hiring someone purely to show off diversity. Avoid this by ensuring every hire is for skills and potential, not just to fill a quota.

- **Avoiding Difficult Conversations:** Not addressing a team member's offensive remark or avoiding discussions on racial inequities doesn't promote inclusivity. Address issues promptly and constructively.

- **Assuming One Size Fits All:** Don't assume what works for one person will work for another. Tailor your management style to individual needs.

In Conclusion

Diversity and inclusion are more than just buzzwords; they are fundamental to building resilient, innovative, and successful teams. As you step into this new leadership role, remember: Embracing D&I is not just about avoiding pitfalls; it's about creating an environment where everyone can thrive. Lead with empathy, understanding, and openness, and you will set the stage for an inclusive culture where every team member feels valued.

Self Care:

How To Really Lead By Example

Welcome to one of the most critical chapters in your journey as a first-time manager. Why, you ask? Because to lead others, one must first learn to lead oneself.

Understanding the Importance of Self-Care

Imagine boarding a flight. As the plane taxis down the runway, the flight attendants demonstrate the safety procedures. They emphasize that in case of an emergency, you should secure your own oxygen mask before assisting others. Why? Because without taking care of yourself first, you may not be able to help anyone else.

Your role as a manager is no different.

The Self-Care Paradox

Being a first-time manager is exhilarating but can also be overwhelming. With increased responsibility and the well-being of a team on your shoulders, it's easy to believe that working late nights and skipping lunches will prove your dedication. But here's a twist: the best leaders prioritize self-care.

Example: Jamie, an enthusiastic new manager, wanted to make a solid impression. She frequently worked through her lunch breaks and stayed late, believing this showed her dedication. Over time, she became exhausted, irritable, and less effective in her decision-making. It wasn't until she began setting aside time for herself that her performance and mood improved.

The Pillars of Self-Care

- **Physical Wellness**: Eat well, exercise, and ensure you get adequate sleep. An active body promotes an active mind.

Example: Raj decided to start his mornings with a 20-minute jog. This not only helped him maintain his health but also allowed him to clear his thoughts and strategize for the day.

- **Mental and Emotional Health**: Seek balance. This means setting boundaries, seeking support when necessary, and practicing mindfulness.

Example: Elena, after facing a particularly challenging week, spoke to her mentor about her feelings of inadequacy. The conversation not only provided perspective but also actionable solutions she could use.

- **Hobbies and Interests**: Don't lose sight of what you love. Whether it's painting, playing an instrument, or hiking, take time to do what makes you happy.

Example: Mike, a new team leader, took an hour each week to indulge in his passion for photography. It became a refreshing escape that also enriched his creativity.

- **Connection**: Spend quality time with loved ones. They provide a supportive system that can help you through challenging times.

Example: Lena made it a rule to have dinner with her family or friends at least three times a week, ensuring she had a break from work and could connect with her loved ones.

The Ripple Effect

As a manager, your behaviour sets the tone for your team. If you're stressed and overwhelmed, your team will feel it. Conversely, if you demonstrate a healthy work-life balance, your team will feel encouraged to do the same.

Example: When Karen, a department head, began taking midday breaks to practice yoga, she noticed her team started to take regular breaks too. Productivity increased, and the overall team morale was noticeably higher.

In Conclusion

As you transition into your management role, remember that leadership is as much about showing as it is about telling. Prioritizing your well-being is not a luxury—it's a necessity. And as you embark on this path of self-care, you'll not only benefit personally but also set an invaluable example for your team.

Remember: To inspire and care for others, start by caring for yourself.

Continuing Your Learning and Growth:

The Developing Leader

As you are now familiar with the essential value of self-care, let's dive into another pivotal facet of leadership: continuous learning and growth. In today's fast-paced world, the concept of "learning and evolving" is not just a fancy catchphrase – it's the backbone of effective leadership.

Why Continuous Learning?

A static leadership approach in a dynamic environment will soon become obsolete. Remember, the world, its technologies, and its challenges are perpetually evolving. Thus, as leaders, we need to evolve too.

Example: Imagine Lucy, who was a wizard at using a particular software five years ago. However, with the rapid emergence of new technologies, her once sought-after skills became outdated. Had Lucy continuously updated her knowledge, she would have maintained her edge.

The Learning Leader's Toolkit

- **Embrace the Learner's Mindset**: Be curious. Adopt the perspective that there is always something new to grasp, no matter how experienced you become.

Example: Jake, a newly promoted manager, didn't shy away from asking questions. He frequently tapped into the expertise of his colleagues, fostering a culture of shared learning.

- **Invest in Professional Development**: Attend workshops, webinars, and conferences. They offer fresh insights and expose you to the latest industry trends.

Example: Amara made it a point to attend at least two industry-specific conferences each year. These not only expanded her network but also provided her with innovative strategies to implement.

- **Read Widely**: Dive into books, articles, or podcasts. Subjects unrelated to your field can also offer diverse perspectives and problem-solving techniques.

Example: Sam, a marketing manager, was an avid fan of psychology and neuroscience books. This interest helped him better understand consumer behaviour and craft more effective campaigns.

- **Seek Feedback**: Constructive feedback, even if tough to swallow, is gold for growth. Welcome it and use it to refine your leadership approach.

Example: Rita initiated monthly feedback sessions with her team. While some comments stung, they provided clarity on areas for improvement, making her a more effective leader.

- **Mentorship and Peer Groups**: Engage with a mentor or join a peer group. Sharing challenges and solutions with those on similar journeys can be enlightening.

Example: Daniel joined a managers' circle in his city, where young leaders met bi-monthly. The collective wisdom of this group helped him navigate many a management storm.

The Ripple Effect of a Learning Leader

Your commitment to learning serves as an unspoken nudge for your team to do the same. A culture of growth and development fosters innovation, adaptability, and resilience.

Example: When Mia introduced a book-of-the-month for her team, it sparked dynamic discussions and fresh ideas. Over time, this small initiative amplified the team's creativity and collaboration.

In Conclusion

Leadership is not a destination but a journey – a journey punctuated with lessons, reflections, and evolutions. As you step into your managerial role, wear your learner's hat with pride. Not only will you evolve as a more adept leader, but you will also inspire your team to be lifelong learners.

Appendix:

Additional Reading & Resources

For First Time Managers

Here, we have compiled a curated list of additional resources, tools, and exercises to aid in your transition into a confident and effective first-time manager. Whether you are looking to dive deeper into a specific topic or seeking practical tools to implement your newfound knowledge, this section has got you covered.

Recommended Reading

- **"Drive: The Surprising Truth About What Motivates Us"** by Daniel H. Pink

    - Understand what really drives motivation and how you can tap into it for your team.

- **"The Five Dysfunctions of a Team: A Leadership Fable"** by Patrick Lencioni

    - A gripping look into the most common pitfalls faced by teams and how to overcome them.

- **"How to Win Friends and Influence People"** by Dale Carnegie

- A classic but timeless piece on human behaviour and effective communication.

- **"Radical Candor: Be a Kick-Ass Boss Without Losing Your Humanity"** by Kim Scott

  - Learn the art of giving feedback and fostering a culture of open communication.

Online Resources

- **Harvard Business Review (HBR)**

  - This premier site has a vast repository of articles on leadership, management, and more. Especially look for their 'New Managers Toolkit'.

- **Myers-Briggs Test (MBTI)**

  - The Myers-Briggs test is used by over 88% of Fortune 500 companies across 115 countries and is an excellent tool to help develop skills of managing a diverse range of personality types.

- **TED Talks on Leadership**

  - Engaging short talks from global leaders providing insights and experiences.

- **MindTools**

  - Offers a range of tools and resources, including management skills assessments, to help you develop further.

Practical Exercises and Tools

- **Self-Reflection Journal**

  - Begin a daily or weekly journal documenting your leadership journey. Note down successes, challenges, and areas of growth.

- **Feedback Surveys**
    - Use platforms like SurveyMonkey or Google Forms to create anonymous feedback surveys for your team. This can give you a pulse on how you are doing.

- **Role-playing Scenarios**
    - With a mentor or fellow manager, role-play challenging situations you might face. This can help you be better prepared for real-life scenarios.

- **Mentorship**
    - Seek out a mentor within your organization or industry who can offer guidance, insights, and feedback on your management journey.

Workshops and Networking Events

- **Toastmasters International**
    - Perfect your public speaking and leadership skills in a local club.

- **Meetup.com**
    - Search for leadership or management groups in your area. These can be great platforms for networking and learning from peers.

- **Chamber of Commerce Events**
    - Often, local chambers host leadership workshops or seminars which can be valuable.

Conclusion

Your Future Awaits

As we reach the end of our shared journey through this book, I am reminded of a fundamental truth: the act of reading and seeking knowledge is in itself a mark of leadership. By choosing to invest in your personal growth and in the future of the teams you will lead, you have taken an essential step toward becoming the leader you aspire to be.

Leading is not just about titles or positions; it's about the daily choices we make, the examples we set, and the relationships we build. Every chapter you have delved into, every lesson you have pondered, has been a testament to your commitment.

In the vast realm of management, there is always more to learn, always new challenges to face. And while this book might mark a conclusion, your leadership journey is just beginning. I hope that the insights, experiences, and principles we have explored together serve as foundational blocks, guiding you as you shape your unique leadership style.

Before we part ways, if you have enjoyed this book or found its content valuable, I would be deeply grateful if you could take a moment to leave a review on Amazon. Your feedback is invaluable. Not only will it assist me in refining future editions, but it will also aid others in discovering and benefiting from the advice contained within these pages.

I want to extend my heartfelt gratitude for allowing me to be a part of your journey. It has been an honour to share with you the lessons I have learned over more than two decades that have shaped my understanding of leadership. Remember, the best leaders aren't just born; they are moulded through experiences, challenges, and a continual quest for knowledge.

Thank you for taking the time to read and for being proactive about your growth. As you move forward, may you inspire, guide, and uplift those around you. Here's to your success, to the amazing teams you will lead, and to the indelible mark you will leave in the world of leadership.

With warm regards and best wishes for your journey ahead,

- *Philip*

www.ingramcontent.com/pod-product-compliance
Lightning Source LLC
Chambersburg PA
CBHW062304290526
45794CB00006B/2697